Original title:
Life's Meaning: A Mystery Wrapped in an Enigma

Copyright © 2025 Creative Arts Management OÜ
All rights reserved.

Author: Juliette Kensington
ISBN HARDBACK: 978-1-80566-264-8
ISBN PAPERBACK: 978-1-80566-559-5

Mysterious Whispers of Dawn

In the morning light, secrets play,
Birds gossip tales, in their own way.
A cat with a sock, oh what a sight,
Pondering shadows, with all its might.

Sunbeams tickle, dew drops giggle,
A squirrel in a hat, oh what a wiggle!
Each blade of grass has a voice to lend,
In this nutty world, there's always a bend.

In the Silence Lies Wisdom

Quiet moments, where thoughts can roam,
A fridge's hum feels like a poem.
Eavesdropping on ants, a philosophical spree,
They argue about crumbs, life's mystery.

Socks left unmatched tell stories untold,
Of friendships formed, both warm and cold.
In stillness we find, with a laugh and a grin,
Questions so wild, where do we begin?

The Stories We Breathe

In every breath, a tale unfolds,
Of winding paths and futures bold.
Chickens laugh, while cows write prose,
Whispers of wisdom in snorts and nos.

The air is thick with giggling sighs,
While ducks share their dreams of the skies.
What can it mean, this chaotic dance?
Maybe it's just a clumsy romance.

Flickering Lights of the Soul

In the dark, fireflies flicker, also blink,
Do they ponder existence, or just wink?
A candle's flame, with a flick and a sway,
Gives sage advice in its own unique way.

Mirrors reflect but can't really see,
The secrets we keep, under the tree.
So let's laugh with the stars and picnic with fate,
Who needs answers? It's all just great!

Uncharted Waters of Emotion

Sailing on waves of wishes rare,
With each splash, there's laughter to share.
Fish wear hats, stars twist in glee,
What's normal here is quite hard to see.

Turtles with ties swim by with flair,
They offer advice, but do we dare?
In this sea of giggles, I float high,
Wondering if squids can tell a good lie.

The Keys to an Unlocked Door

I found some keys that jingle and shine,
But none fit the locks that truly are mine.
A cat in a bowler gives me a wink,
Should I trust it, or just rethink?

Behind every door, there's a doorbell that sings,
And inside are the dreams of strange-looking things.
A sofa that bakes cookies, a rug with a grin,
In this wild house, where do I begin?

The Search for Forgotten Echoes

Echoes of giggles float through the air,
They vanish too fast, but I don't despair.
I chase them with marshmallows and glee,
Yet they just laugh and flee from me.

Each step I take leads to a dance,
With echoes that twirl in a strange little prance.
Whispers of wisdom—what could they be?
Just my socks arguing where they want to flee.

Dancing Shadows on the Wall

Shadows take tango lessons at night,
With a gentle flicker, they spin with delight.
A toaster joins in, it's a sight to behold,
With bread in its pocket, it's graceful and bold.

The moon plays the piano, oh what a tune!
As shadows and pastries dance under the moon.
I sit back in awe, with a pie on my lap,
Wondering if shadows ever take a nap.

Fragments of a Forgotten Tale

In shadows dance the quirky sprites,
With jumbled thoughts and silly fights.
They giggle loud, they twist and twirl,
Each secret shared, a puzzling whirl.

A loaf of bread in fairy's play,
Might just hold secrets, or a stray!
The breadcrumbs lead to wobbly paths,
Where laughter echoes, nothing lasts.

The Allure of the Unknown

What lurks beyond the curtain's fold?
A sock, a shoe, or tales retold?
The office chair might just take flight,
And spin you 'round past dot of light.

The fridge hums secrets in the night,
Of leftovers lost in endless flight.
If you dare peek, what will you find?
Perhaps just crumbs, or noodles timed!

Life as a Riddle

If riddles come with playful bits,
Then why do socks create such fits?
The cat looks wise, yet chases dust,
Solving how to nap is a must.

Through questions asked, and answers skipped,
I bought some beans, my wallet dipped.
Yet laughter fills each puzzling turn,
For joy's the quest, from which we learn.

Unspoken

Whispers of shadows walk the line,
Where nothing is as it seems divine.
The plot thickens like a morning stew,
And every flavor's oddly new.

Why do we ponder, why do we seek?
The answer's silly, hiding meek.
We laugh and swirl in tangled ways,
Where silent giggles fill our days.

The Journey Through the Veil

Step through the mist, it's just a game,
Where cotton candy writes your name.
The world's a stage, the curtain taut,
With every scene, a lesson sought.

Adventures wait beyond the sigh,
Of what we thought would surely fly.
So come along, bring your best hat,
For mysteries bloom where laughter's at.

Whispers of the Unseen

In a world of questions seen,
The cat's out, but where's the queen?
Cabbages talk, or so they say,
Yet no one listens in the fray.

A shadow dances with a grin,
It tickles thoughts beneath the skin.
The cake of truth is half undone,
Who baked it, though? We're still not done.

A squirrel spills the cosmic beans,
While washing up in rainbow streams.
The stars just wink and wave hello,
While earthly woes put on a show.

So let's pretend we understand,
As rubber ducks take over land.
In giggles, we'll embrace the strange,
For mysteries love a little change.

The Puzzle of Existence

Jigsaw pieces of the day,
Crammed in boxes tossed in play.
A turtle trips, laughs like a fool,
Chasing thoughts, we just can't spool.

Why does the toaster pop with glee,
While washing socks sets the cat free?
Giraffes wear ties to coffee shops,
Spilling secrets, that never stops.

The moon has socks to match its shoes,
And coffee waves its arms like news.
In this circus, we all want a turn,
To crack the code and watch it burn.

So grab a riddle, twist your brain,
A dance of questions with no refrain.
We'll roll the dice, let laughter reign,
In this wild world that feels just plain.

Shadows of the Soul

Shadows wiggle in the light,
Chasing thoughts like kites in flight.
A gnome recites the rules of fun,
While shopping carts make a run.

Pirates argue with the breeze,
Over treasures hidden in trees.
A panda eats with such fine grace,
Who knew that naps could win this race?

Glasses clink in silly cheers,
As fish gossip about their peers.
What's real, what's fake? Who's keeping score?
A ticklish laugh from behind the door.

So let's adorn our minds with stripes,
And dance among the silly types.
For in this game, we play our roles,
With jests and jives in shadowed strolls.

Beneath the Veil of Being

Underneath that goofy hat,
A talking duck shares tales of chat.
Why do crickets sing at night?
To dazzle dreams with sheer delight.

A dinner plate explains the quirks,
Of broccoli with superhero works.
The calendar slips on a banana,
Time giggles with a hint of drama.

The sirens call in parrot song,
As chaos hums a silly gong.
In rubber boots, we wade through rhymes,
Creating treasure out of crimes.

So here we sit, with jester's glee,
In this grand game of you and me.
Why take it serious, let's be friends,
For the mystery laughs, and never ends.

Between Stars and Silence

In the void where whispers twirl,
Stars giggle, cosmic pearls.
Is it ketchup or is it fate?
Floating thoughts, why not wait?

Gravitational laughs collide,
Aliens dance, nosh and hide.
With sandwich dreams, they all conspire,
Wishing for a cosmic choir.

Rocket ships with wonky wings,
Play hide and seek with cosmic flings.
A donut in the twilight spark,
Navigating through the dark.

Between the stars, life lingers here,
With comets that chortle, full of cheer.
What's the score on this grand play?
A cosmic joke, or just cliché?

The Labyrinth of Thought

In a maze of twists and turns,
Where reason simmers and churns.
I lost my keys, it's quite absurd,
Chasing answers, truth deferred.

The walls are sticky with gooey quests,
Finding meaning in misplaced jest.
Did I trip on a thought or two?
Or was it that last taco stew?

A ball of yarn unraveled fast,
An idea that couldn't quite last.
I pondered deep, but came up blank,
The universe just giggled, prank.

Frantically seeking crumbs of sense,
While dancing with my own pretense.
A riddle wrapped in sock-clad feet,
Perhaps answering is incomplete.

Secrets in the Mirror

Gazing deep into reflective sheen,
What's lurking there? You've seen the scene.
A goofy grin, a twinkling eye,
Did my reflection just sigh?

It whispers tales of what could be,
A banana peel calls, 'Dance with me!'
Frogs in tuxedos leap and croak,
Their laughter charges, a silly joke.

Am I the one who's in control?
Or just a puppet in a troll's scroll?
With each glance, a new riddle spins,
Is the truth hiding underneath my skin?

The mirror chuckles, winks with glee,
It knows the secrets of you and me.
I'm a puzzle, puzzling still,
But laughter? Oh, what a thrill!

A Journey Through the Abyss

Down a hole that seems so deep,
Past the echoes, secrets creep.
With a pizza box, I took the dive,
Wondering if I'd come out alive.

Monsters dance with socks askew,
In the dark, who knew?
Baffled by their savage glee,
A disco party just for me!

Shadows prance, knocking chairs,
"Don't take life too serious, who cares?"
Diving deeper, the laughter rolls,
Are we simply jokes with beating souls?

Through the abyss, mysteries whiz,
Where questions boil, and humor is fizz.
I've cracked the code, or was it a game?
In the end, we're all the same.

The Essence of Paradox

In the circus of our days, we spin,
Clowns and scholars mix in joyful din.
Balancing dreams on stilts so tall,
We laugh at the falls, but who has the ball?

Whispers of wisdom dressed as jest,
The riddle of existence puts us to the test.
Finding truth in a punchline shared,
The search for the light often feels so rare.

With every tick-tock of the clock so grand,
We juggle the moments, an awkward band.
The punchline hits hard, yet we're all unsure,
Is it folly or fortune that we all endure?

So wear your bright smile and don your red nose,
Embrace the paradox, for who really knows?
In the absurdity, we find our route,
In laughter, we dance, chasing shadows about.

Mirrors of the Soul's Journey

Reflective puddles show the way,
Dancing raindrops giggle and sway.
We study our faces, all askew,
In these strange mirrors, is that really you?

A twisted path of wondrous quirks,
The road to knowing is full of jerks.
Each step a riddle, wrapped in a shoe,
The theories we hold, keep changing too.

We gather our thoughts like cats on a fence,
Trying to ponder with no common sense.
Suddenly wise, then stupid again,
The path to clarity is a slippery vein.

But still we wander with no fixed aim,
Chasing reflections in this silly game.
For every mirror that shows us a face,
Holds something different in our cosmic space.

Beneath Clay and Stars

Beneath our feet lies a cosmic scheme,
With ants on a mission, and stones with a dream.
Each speck of dirt speaks tales from the past,
While stars above giggle, it all goes so fast.

The cosmos winks, a capricious friend,
Molding our fates, on it we depend.
Planting gardens of thought in soil so black,
Up to the heavens, we both give and lack.

With roots entangled, we're all in this mess,
Each moment a giggle, a cosmic caress.
Digging for answers is such a delight,
We play hide and seek, both day and night.

So toast to the clay, and lift up your cup,
For the stars and the bugs all play in our up.
In the earth's grand ballet, we twirl and we spin,
Who knew mud could hold such a treasure within?

The Chronicles of Fleeting Shadows

Fleeting shadows dance in the glow,
Chasing after dawn's comedic show.
Here one moment, then slipping away,
The secrets they hold are quite here to stay.

Tickling our thoughts like feathers so light,
They flit through our days, both silly and bright.
We ponder their essence, as they disappear,
The folly of time is the punchline, I fear.

In this shadowy tale, we laugh through the tears,
As moments collude to confound our fears.
Yet still we find joy in the fleeting and fun,
In shadows we whisper, our journey's begun.

So let's spin with the shadows, let's dance with the night,
For every brief flicker contains pure delight.
The chronicles whisper of laughter and woe,
In the world of the shadows, our spirits will glow.

The Dance of Uncertainty

In a world of twists and turns,
We're dancing shoes with paper burns.
Each step's a guess, a chance, a laugh,
As we tango with the aftermath.

With partners who have two left feet,
We sway to rhythms bittersweet.
Is it waltz or just a jig?
We laugh at truths that seem so big.

The music plays, but no one knows,
If it's the end or just a pose.
We leap and twirl, yet still confuse,
The scoreboard's blank; we're free to choose.

So let's embrace this grand charade,
With silly hats and wild parade.
For in this dance of oddity,
Who needs a clue? Just dance with me!

Fragments of a Hidden Truth

In every puzzle, pieces stray,
We hunt for meaning day by day.
A sock, a shoe, a spoon or two,
What's the point? We haven't a clue!

A cat with wisdom, tail held high,
Laughs at us as we wonder why.
We sift through crumbs of nonsense low,
Perhaps the truth is stuck in stow.

Like Sherlock's hat hanging askew,
The secrets whisper, 'Here's a view!'
We chase the echoes of our thoughts,
But answers seem to tie in knots.

Yet here we sit, with giggles bright,
In fragments lost, we still find light.
For every riddle that we miss,
We find a chance for comic bliss!

Chasing Shadows and Silhouettes

In a realm where shadows play,
We chase their forms throughout the day.
Like puppets dancing on a wall,
Are they real or just a call?

With every step, a playful tease,
They shift and twist, as if to please.
We run, we trip, we laugh aloud,
At shadows acting like a crowd.

A silhouette of doubt and cheer,
Whispers secrets for all to hear.
Is that a ghost or just my mate?
Who needs the truth when life's so great!

So let's embrace these ghostly friends,
For laughter's glow never quite ends.
In chasing shadows, we won't fret,
For mystery's fun, you can bet!

Enigmas in Every Breath

Take a breath, it's full of quirks,
Like random darts that miss their marks.
Each gasp's a riddle, oh so sweet,
With questions none can quite repeat.

The air is thick with what-ifs and whys,
As brain cells dance and syllables rise.
Just when we think we found the key,
A gust of wind says, 'Not so free!'

With every inhale, laughter blooms,
A world of charm in twisted rooms.
From fleeting thoughts that zoom past fast,
We giggle at the questions cast.

So breathe it in, the mystery clear,
With chuckles bright, we hold it near.
For in each breath, a quirk awaits,
And isn't that what really creates?

The Puzzle of the Solitary Heart

A heart once sat with missing piece,
It looked quite lonely, but not at least.
With jigsaw shapes and colors bright,
It searched for love, by day and night.

It tried a cat, it tried a dog,
But they just wagged, like them a fog.
In kitchen pots and spoons it sought,
But only found a moldy thought.

One day it met a quirky shoe,
They laughed and danced, a perfect view.
The heart then learned, to its delight,
That missing pieces sometimes bite.

So now it fills with socks and hats,
A cozy mess with shoes and chats.
With laughter shared, it feels so smart,
The puzzle's fun, not just an art.

Echoes of a Silent Dream

In slumber deep, a dream did creep,
It whispered secrets, not too steep.
A frog in tie, a dance so grand,
He boogied on with a wobbly hand.

The echoes bounced from wall to wall,
Tickling thoughts, both big and small.
A burger crowned, a crown of fries,
The dream just laughed, to my surprise.

Yet in the morn, it took its leave,
Like socks that vanish, just to grieve.
But I still chuckle, what a scheme,
For in that night, was quite the dream.

So if you hear a giggle loud,
From restless dreams, feel quite proud.
It means a froggy stole the scene,
And danced away, what a routine!

Threads of the Unraveled

In a world of yarn, a knitter sat,
With tangled threads, and purring cat.
She wove a tale of socks and hats,
But soon she found, she got the bats!

The fabric stretched, then did a twist,
A rainbow loop that couldn't resist.
Her projects danced and sang a song,
A bowling ball—what could go wrong?

She laughed and cried at what she spun,
A sweater knit for everyone.
But then it grew, three sizes more,
A monster hug she can't ignore.

Now every friend wears Billy's coat,
With threads so wild, like boats afloat.
And they all glare in joyful fright,
At what began as pure delight!

Secrets Beneath the Surface

The fish swims round with curious glee,
He plots and plans, for what might be.
Beneath the waves, he caught a wink,
A mermaid's laugh, oh what to think!

They snickered at the sunken chest,
Filled with chips, a pirate's fest.
With goldfish snacks and treasure cold,
The secrets shared, a tale retold.

They danced on currents, swirled with flair,
Through bubble parties, without a care.
But all at once, they dropped their bait,
A toaster popped, they couldn't wait.

So here's to fish with dreams so fine,
That dive for snacks, and sip some wine.
In water deep, they dream and cheer,
For secrets shared bring summer near!

The Enigma Beneath the Surface

Beneath the calm, a riddle sleeps,
With socks that vanish, laughter creeps.
Where do they go, those cotton foes?
Are they off to join a dance that glows?

In kitchen drawers, the spoons conspire,
To hide the forks, they never tire.
What's brewing here, a plot or show?
An epic tale of dinner woe!

The cat sits high, a furry lord,
While dogs debate their goofy reward.
What's on their minds, oh, what a treat?
Chasing shadows or perhaps a meat?

Yet underneath the giggles lie,
The truths we seek beneath the sky.
Join the quest, don't be a bore,
For mysteries wait behind each door!

Questions Lost in Time

What's the shape of a butterfly's dream?
Or why do we always lose our keys, it seems?
Is chocolate a fruit, can it take flight?
Or just a sweet joke that fuels midnight?

Ticking clocks hold secrets so grand,
While mismatched socks play in a band.
Do the stars giggle when we look away?
Or roll their eyes at our clumsy sway?

Toasters pop bread, but where does it go?
Is it visiting toast land, or just for show?
And if doughnuts have holes, what do they hide?
A space for dreams or sugar's pride?

So question away, let laughter flow,
In this peculiar world where oddities grow.
For the answers, dear friend, we may never find,
But that's the fun, being perplexed and blind!

The Silhouette of Solitude

In shadows cast by my mirror's glow,
I dance alone, a solo show.
With my trusty brush, I paint the night,
Creating birds that take to flight.

What do clouds think of when they float?
Do they whisper secrets in a gossamer coat?
Or do they ponder what's for lunch today?
A sprinkle of rain or sun's warm play?

The fridge hums softly, what does it know?
It keeps my leftovers, it holds the flow.
Are they reminiscing on their finest days?
Or dreaming of feasts in fanciful ways?

So here I sit, with oversized dreams,
In the silliness of silence, nothing seems.
Yet within this quiet, joy sneaks in,
For solitude sings, and it feels like a win!

Whispers from the Infinite

The moon winks at me from a velvet sea,
As planets debate, 'What's the best tea?'
Do comets gossip as they streak and spin?
Or ponder if travelers ever will win?

Galaxies twirl like ballerinas at play,
Creating new worlds by night and by day.
What do they think of our Earthly fuss?
With traffic jams and trains that discuss!

If stars could giggle, oh what a sound,
As they watch us trip on the ground.
Perhaps they chuckle at our grand displays,
Of chasing our tails in mysterious ways!

So let's toast to the cosmos, both silly and vast,
With questions unending, forever we'll cast.
For in this boundless dance, we find delight,
In the myriad mysteries that twinkle at night!

Navigating through Fog and Clarity

In the morning, I sip my tea,
While pondering where I wander, you see.
The clouds giggle, they tease my mind,
As I trip over thoughts that are quite intertwined.

The squirrels conspire in the trees,
Whispering secrets on the breeze.
I laugh at their antics, so wild and spry,
While I'm lost in the maze of the why and the sigh.

The sun peeks through, a sly little grin,
As I question if this is where I begin.
A compass spins, a map made of cheese,
Who knew chasing answers would be such a tease?

Yet in this fog, a spark shines bright,
With each wrong turn, I find new delight.
From riddles and puzzles, I take my cue,
It's the circus of wonder and nonsense anew!

The Silent Voice Within

I hear a whisper deep in my head,
It tells me daily to carry my bread.
But is it a thought or just my old sock?
I'm torn between wisdom and my morning clock.

The muffins in the oven start to sing,
While I'm pondering the meaning of everything.
Is it the cake mix or my brain-baked dreams?
These answers are hidden, or so it seems.

But maybe it's laughter I seek in the air,
With all the quirky animals, everywhere.
I try to decipher that giggling muse,
Who'd have thought wisdom wears multicolored shoes?

So here I stand, a puzzle to crack,
With laughter as the guide, I won't look back.
Through tales of the silly and unplanned delight,
I'll dance with confusion, from morning to night!

The Enchanted Passage of Time

Tick-tock goes the silly old clock,
Which insists that I dance, and then take stock.
It winks and it nods, with mischief in eye,
But I'm late for my meeting with a cake in the sky.

Days flutter past like bright little birds,
Chirping in rhymes, slipping past without words.
I juggle my hours, with a grin and a spin,
Whether losing or winning, it's all part of the din.

If time is a puzzle best left incomplete,
Then I'll wear mismatched socks, oh what a feat!
As marbles roll down, I'll gather them near,
For I'm simply collecting what's 'fun' and sincere.

So here's to the minutes, both silly and grand,
With cake and confetti at my command.
In this strange passage, where days intertwine,
I'll chase after moments, so sweet and divine!

Hidden Pathways of the Heart

In a garden of giggles, my heart starts to roam,
With petunias and daisies, it feels like home.
I follow the butterflies, drawn to their dance,
And wonder if butterflies dream of romance.

Yet paths twist and turn, in whimsical ways,
Leading me down to a land filled with plays.
Where hearts are like puzzles, all mixed up true,
And laughter's the glue that binds me to you.

I stumble on truths, like pebbles of light,
They shine when you find them, oh what a sight!
In secret cove corners where shadows do swirl,
A treasure of joy tucked away in a whirl.

So here's to the pathways, both silly and bright,
Where hearts find their rhythm and dance in the night.
As I wander these mazes, I'm giggling from start,
For every new turn leads me back to the heart.

The Symphony of Uncertainty

In a world of twists and turns,
The purpose hides and yearns.
We dance to tunes we cannot hear,
While juggling dreams and a can of beer.

With each note played, we laugh and sigh,
Guessing motives as days go by.
The conductor's lost, or maybe late,
But what's the rush? Let's celebrate!

We wear our masks and spin around,
In this circus of the profound.
With popcorn in hand, we take a seat,
To watch the show that's bittersweet.

So here's to the chaos, cheerfully spun,
In this grand performance, we're all just one.
With a wink and a grin, let's raise our glass,
For the symphony plays, and we'll let it pass.

Threads of Light in Darkness

In shadows deep, we weave our thread,
With laughter ringing in our head.
We search for that glint, a spark of truth,
While stubbing toes on the fountain of youth.

Tangled paths and silly fights,
Illuminating dark and starry nights.
With each misstep, a stitch we make,
Creating patterns from the mistakes.

The more we ponder, the less we know,
But in our confusion, we steal the show.
The light breaks through, a curious dance,
In this tapestry of happenstance.

So let's embrace the tangled mess,
With all its flaws, we'll still impress.
A patchwork life is ours to wear,
In our colorful fabric, we find a flare.

The Theater of Existence

We take the stage with floppy shoes,
In a play of chaos, reading cues.
The script is strange, the plot absurd,
Who wrote this? Oh, I'm not sure!

The curtain rises, the lights go dim,
With each mishap, we laugh and grin.
The audience claps, unsure what to feel,
As we juggle truths with a touch of zeal.

Dramatic pauses and silly plays,
We question our roles in countless ways.
With a wink to fate, we blunder, we trip,
As the spotlight gleams on every slip.

So take a bow, we're all in this show,
In the theater of life, the laughs overflow.
Whether tragedy or comedy, who can say?
Just grab your popcorn, enjoy the display!

Chasing the Shadows

With shadow puppets at our side,
We chase the dark with arms open wide.
We play hide and seek with what's unseen,
In this game of life, we laugh and preen.

The shadows giggle, they dance with glee,
As we stumble along, just trying to be.
We throw our hands up, giving our all,
In this silly dance, we sometimes fall.

Questions swirl in darkened nooks,
While we pretend to read the books.
With every leap, we risk the fall,
But what's the fun if we stand tall?

So chase those shadows, let's laugh and play,
In this glorious chaos, we'll find our way.
With pokes and prods, we'll uncover the jest,
In chasing the shadows, we're truly blessed.

The Cloak of Mystery

In shadows dance the thoughts we chase,
Like socks that vanish without a trace.
We ponder hard, with furrowed brow,
Yet what's the answer? No one knows how!

With every riddle, we scratch our heads,
While questions float like airy breads.
I ask the cat, but it just meows,
Is wisdom hidden in fuzzy brows?

We search for truths beneath the stars,
As clowns in life, driving flashy cars.
With coffee cups and silly hats,
We giggle, ponder—how absurd is that?

In this grand show, we play our part,
With laughter echoing in the heart.
So join the dance, don't miss your cue,
For in this game, the jest is you!

The Echo of Forgotten Questions

When did we begin to wonder so?
Was it at birth, or long ago?
Were we rock stars in a previous life?
Or did we just misplace the kitchen knife?

The questions linger in the air,
Like odd socks without a pair.
Do ducks really quack just to be loud?
And why does coffee make us proud?

Oh time, you sneaky little thief,
Stealing moments, yet granting relief.
We chase the answers like a dog to a bone,
While giggling alone, just like a drone.

So let them echo, these silly thoughts,
As we ponder while cooking pots.
For in confusion, humor blooms,
As we dance across the crowded rooms!

The Veins of an Infinite Story

Stories flow like rivers wide,
With twists and turns, the tide will ride.
We scribble notes on napkin scraps,
While dreaming up with silly claps.

Each tale's a billboard, loud and bright,
Filled with laughter, sparks, and slight fright.
But in the end, what's really true?
A mermaid's song or a cat in a shoe?

Tales of heroes and quests unfold,
Bold adventures and secrets told.
Yet sometimes it's just… my shoe's lost a lace,
In this wild, peculiar human race.

So we'll keep spinning this web of fun,
With crazy plots beneath the sun.
Each moment captures the laughter's flow,
Entwined in a story we all should know!

Paths Crossing Under the Moon

Met at midnight under the bright sphere,
Where dreams get tossed and lost in cheer.
We stumble upon new friends and jest,
In the glow of the moon, we feel blessed.

What brings us here? Who can say?
A hodgepodge of chance, in a silly way.
With stories shared, we laugh and tease,
As stars above twinkle with ease.

Life's a journey, a zigzagging ride,
With paths that cross where laughter's applied.
So take my hand, let's hop and skip,
Through this cosmic, whimsical trip.

As the moon grins down, with a wink so sly,
We toast to the moments that float by.
For in every step, let joy abide,
Under the moon, let dreams collide!

The Canvas of Existence

On a canvas splashed with hues,
Brushstrokes dance, a lively muse.
Colors clash, then blend and play,
Making sense in a wacky way.

A cat with glasses, sipping tea,
Ponders why the world could be.
Juggling thoughts like balls of yarn,
Finding joy in every turn.

In a carnival of dreams we ride,
With ticklish thoughts we cannot hide.
A rollercoaster of giggles, fast,
Each twist and turn a blast from the past.

So grab a brush and join the fun,
With splashes wild, our work's begun.
Who knew art could be so bright?
With laughter paint the day and night!

Reflections in the Twilight

In twilight's glow, the shadows prance,
As questions whirl in a silly dance.
Do fish wear shoes? Do cows like cheese?
With thoughts like these, we laugh and tease.

A mirror shows a face quite strange,
With mismatched socks, well, isn't that range?
Who are we in this light so odd?
Just jesters here, with wisdom clawed.

As stars appear, they blink and wink,
Do they ponder too, or just drink pink?
A gathering of lights with stories to share,
In this cosmic circus, we all have flair.

So let's toast to the silly and absurd,
To ponder the quirks without a word.
Twilight's jokes we'll never solve,
In this playful riddle, we dissolve.

The Labyrinth of Thought

In the maze of thought, I took a stroll,
Chasing rabbits, what a toll!
Did you hear the one about a shoe?
It walked right off, as shoes often do.

Around each corner, a riddle does tease,
Why do we argue with the breeze?
Thoughts spin like tops, round and round,
In this tangled web, what's lost is found.

A monkey wearing a hat of cheese,
Sips on a smoothie, just for ease.
"Why is it all so flippin' whack?"
Maybe thoughts just like to snack.

So laugh along as we twist and turn,
In this thought maze, there's much to learn.
From silly clues to punchlines' worth,
This labyrinth knows the heart's true mirth.

Veils of Wonder

Behind the veil, a rabbit grins,
With pockets full of woes and whims.
He checks his watch; it's tea time now,
But first, a dance—oh, take a bow!

A magic hat, a jester's riddle,
Fluffy clouds play an off-key fiddle.
What's under that veil, you ask with glee?
A world of wonders, wild as can be!

Mirrors twist in giggles and sights,
Jokes that spin through days and nights.
Peeking through laughter, we slowly find,
The joy of wonder frames the mind.

So lift the veil, let's share a jest,
In the garden of smiles, we feel the best.
With every chuckle, our hearts align,
In this tangled web, our spirits shine!

An Odyssey of Questions

Why do socks always disappear?
Is the universe a giant sneeze?
Do fish ever get thirsty?
Or do they swim with such ease?

Why do we park on driveways?
And yet, we drive on the park?
Do cats plot to take over?
While leaving us in the dark?

Do candles wish for more light?
Would mushrooms dance if they could?
Is laughter just oxygen?
Boiling over like good food?

So, let's wander in this maze,
With smiles to light our way.
For in the end, it appears,
Questions are fun to play!

The Heartbeat of the Unseen

What makes a sandwich a meal?
Is cereal soup, or a snack?
When do forgotten dreams spin?
And ask us to take them back?

Does time truly have a grip?
Or is it like stretchy cheese?
Do bananas have much fun?
When they're prancing in the breeze?

Is the sun just a big bulb?
Hanging out on a blue stage?
Will robots ever ponder?
When they're gone to that last page?

In this jest of hidden thoughts,
Laughter wraps the unknown tight.
Each heartbeat whispers secrets,
That dance in the pale moonlight.

Clouds of Confusion

Why do we never see owls?
When they say they're quite awake?
Is bread really a comfort?
Or just a loaf-shaped heartache?

Do shadows dream of sunlight?
Or are they just fearsome friends?
If coffee asked for a hug,
Would we spill it as it blends?

Is there a club for lost keys?
And do they hold secret meets?
Do whispers carry the weight,
Of all our silly defeats?

Let's frolic through these odd thoughts,
With giggles and playful charms.
For clouds may block the sunshine,
But not our joyful alarms!

Journey into the Abyss

What if doors are just a tease?
With secrets that swing just so?
Do pencils dream of their lead?
Or fly when we don't know?

Are socks just a quest for mates?
They disappear without a trace?
Do aliens find us amusing?
As we wander through this space?

Is laughter the glue of the brave?
Or just a trick of the light?
Do we travel in loops, you see?
When aiming for the height?

In this spiral of whimsical thought,
We dance with a grin on our face.
For every odd little mystery,
Brings joy to our classic chase!

The Unseen Currents of Fate

In shadows sly, our thoughts take flight,
Like socks that vanish, out of sight.
The toast that lands, butter-first,
Suggests chaos rules, we're all well-versed.

We chase our dreams with silly glee,
Like cats who think they own the tree.
But each mishap, a twist of fate,
Turns weighty woes to laughs, just wait!

We build our castles, just of sand,
With jellybeans, that's our grand plan.
In twilight's glow, we close one eye,
And giggle at stars that wave goodbye.

So let's embrace the wobbly ride,
Like waltzing ducks, we dance, we glide.
In each small stumble, we find the cheer,
For mysteries wrap us, year after year.

Secrets of the Eclipsed Star

A starry night, a shadowed show,
Secrets hidden, in cosmic glow.
The aliens laugh and roll their eyes,
At humans lost in their own sighs.

With every pause, a riddle tight,
Why do splashes seem so bright?
We ponder deep on matters small,
Like why does the cat ignore our call?

Galaxies spin like cotton candy,
While we chase dreams, sometimes uncanny.
With popcorn kernels popping loud,
We wonder if fate's just a clown proud.

So grab a drink, perhaps a snack,
And laugh at thoughts that tend to crack.
In starlit skies, let's celebrate,
The silly secrets that we create.

The Whispering Wind of Change

The winds do whisper tales anew,
Of mismatched socks and last week's stew.
They carry giggles, not just strife,
With hints of what a wild day's life.

Each gust can toss our hats around,
And send us tumbling to the ground.
Yet in the swirl, there's joy we find,
Like ice cream cones left unconfined.

We'll ride the breezes, see where they steer,
With maps made out of dreams and cheer.
They'll lead us to puddles, made of fate,
Where splashes jump and we participate.

So laugh at change, embrace the breeze,
And dance like leaves that swirl with ease.
For in each gust, a secret prance,
Awaits the brave who love to dance.

A Playful Dance with the Unknown

In shadows where the quirks reside,
We tango with fate, it's a fun ride.
With silly hats and shoes that squeak,
We find the answers we dare to seek.

The unknown winks with a cheeky grin,
It invites us in, let the dance begin.
With every twirl, a giggle escapes,
Like a puppy chasing its own tail shapes.

We step on toes, the rhythm's absurd,
Yet the laughter echoes, joy is stirred.
A haze of mystery drapes the floor,
While confusion joins us, we ask for more.

So grab a partner, let's spin away,
In this zany dance, we choose to play.
With each misstep, we push ahead,
In the waltz of wonder, our hearts are led.

The Unveiling of Tomorrow

Tomorrow comes with socks askew,
With giggles hiding from the view.
A cat walks by with knowing grace,
And time just bobs like it's in a race.

Each dawn brings choices, oh so bright,
Like choosing cake or a pillow fight.
We slip on dreams, a little tight,
Then spin around, what a delight!

A tangle of thoughts in choppy seas,
We laugh and dance with evening breeze.
The clock may tick, but we just sway,
Enjoying every quirky day.

So grab your shades, let's run outside,
With clumsy steps and hearts that glide.
The mystery's here; we take it slow,
In tangled joys, we gleefully flow.

Moments Wrapped in Stillness

In silence, quirks and giggles bloom,
As shadows stretch beneath the moon.
A loaf of bread sprouts tiny legs,
While toast is dancing, what a dregs!

Laughter echoes through the trees,
As squirrels plot against the bees.
The stillness hums a quirky tune,
With secrets hiding in the rune.

Clouds turn shapes of wacky grace,
A flying fish, a backward face.
We pause to ponder, what is chance?
Then join the clouds in silly dance.

In quiet moments, fun ignites,
With silly thoughts on fuzzy nights.
Wrapped in joy, we can't resist,
A wink from fate, we laugh and twist.

The Interwoven Threads of Fate

Threads of fate can tickle toes,
With tangled yarn, it grows and grows.
A funny hat upon your head,
In this strange weave, we laugh instead.

We chase the dreams that curl and twirl,
Like spaghetti in a dizzy whirl.
Each choice a stitch, both bold and bright,
Stitched with laughter, oh what a sight!

The weaving looms with colors rare,
A tapestry adorned with flair.
We pluck the threads with cheerful tease,
Creating chaos, if you please.

As patterns fade and colors clash,
We giggle through our silly splash.
In fate's embrace, we joyously float,
In webbed hilarity, we happily gloat.

Beauty Behind the Disguise

Behind the mask, there's laughter loud,
A playful wink from nature's crowd.
A tree may chat in whispers sweet,
While daisies wear their fancy feet.

The world's a stage with costumes bright,
A jester's dance in morning light.
With funny hats and mismatched shoes,
We giggle as we spread the news.

A comet streaks with a silly grin,
Chasing thoughts that twirl and spin.
The universe will wink and nod,
While we embrace the whimsical odd.

So lift your eyes, let levity soar,
In each disguise, there's so much more.
With joy that twinkles from within,
The beauty hides in every grin.

The Heartbeat of Paradoxes

In a land where socks mate, it's true,
I searched for answers, and found a shoe.
The cat on the counter, the dog in the chair,
Spoke secrets of wisdom, while I just stare.

Why is it the more I seek the wise,
The more I trip over mismatched ties?
Yet laughter echoes in corners of doubt,
As I juggle the mysteries, roundabout.

Each step is a puzzle, a riddle to crack,
With each twist and turn, there's no looking back.
So let's dance with paradox, and grin with glee,
For nothing's more certain than uncertainty!

Oh, the fruitcake's a metaphor, can't you see?
A slice of confusion served joyfully.
In a world full of oddities, I'll take my chance,
With a laugh and a twirl in this silly romance.

Illusions of the Every Day

A coffee cup whispers in morning serenades,
While the toast jumps up, in a buttery parade.
With every spilled secret, the floors get sticky,
As the clock ticks loudly, just acting tricky.

The fridge hums a tune of sweet, cold delight,
While the plants giggle softly, tucked in for the night.
Hey, who turned the lights off? Is it me or the cat?
In this circus of daily acts, imagine that!

Each mundane moment's a whimsical jest,
Like a sock that ain't single—who's truly the best?
Life's quirks are a dance, so let's waltz down the lane,
With each stumble and laugh, nothing is plain.

Why does the spoon get jealous of forks?
As the cereal leaps and the milk quietly borks.
In this comedy show called the present, dear friend,
Let's revel in madness—there's no way to end!

Whispers of the Infinite

Stars in the sky have some stories to tell,
While the moon winks knowingly—oh, very well!
What if the clouds are just giant cotton balls?
And rainbows are trails of joy from the falls?

The universe chuckles in riddles and rhymes,
While squirrels debate the best nutty crimes.
As I ponder the cosmos with a slice of pie,
Do aliens sip lattes, or just silently fly?

Questions like these keep my mind in a spin,
Like a cat chasing shadows, where does it begin?
Frogs have the answers, as they jump with flair,
Croaking the secrets of why we're all here.

Each ponderous thought is just a ticklish tease,
How many licks, till we understand ease?
With giggles of stardust, I float in delight,
Let's dance with the wonders, till morning is bright.

Shadows of the Unseen Path

As shadows play tag with the flickering light,
I trip over thoughts that just might take flight.
Ghosts of old questions giggle around,
Tripping my sneakers with whispers profound.

What if my fears are just silliness dressed?
An octopus dancing in a colorful fest?
Imagine the worries as rubbery bugs,
That bounce on the walls, like loveable thugs!

The road is a puzzle with curveballs galore,
With hiccups of laughter, who could ask for more?
Each twist is a chance to flip the script right,
On this journey of chuckles, we laugh in the night.

So let's embrace shadows like friends at a show,
And see where the whimsy continues to flow.
For in every stumblin', slip, and delightful spree,
Lies a mystery of joy waiting for me.

The Dance of Fleeting Moments

In the hustle and the bustle, we twirl and spin,
Chasing after laughter, let the fun begin.
A tickle in the air, a wink from the sun,
We dance through confusion, oh what a run!

The clock keeps ticking, but who really cares?
We juggle all our worries, like colorful bears.
With every silly stumble, we laugh harder still,
In this merry madness, we find our thrill.

Moments like bubbles, they pop and they glow,
Each one a riddle, we take on the show.
With every quick step, the answers elude,
Yet we chase the absurd, and that's quite shrewd!

So strap on your shoes, let's tango with time,
In this comical chaos, we find our rhyme.
Though the puzzle's a puzzle, we waltz with style,
Finding joy in the mystery, all the while.

Beneath Stars, Beyond Time

Under a sky painted in sparkles and beams,
We ponder the cosmos and dance in our dreams.
What's up with those stars? They're twinkling with glee,
Do they share our secrets, or sip cosmic tea?

Gathered around fires, with marshmallows near,
We roast our deep thoughts with laughter and cheer.
Time's just a notion, a playful charade,
As we chase shooting stars, our worries all fade.

With gravity's pull, we wobble, we sway,
Every question we ponder, tossed far away.
The universe winks, hiding more than it shows,
Yet here in this moment, our silliness grows.

So let's reach for the stars, and tickle the moon,
With giggles and grins, we'll burst into tune.
For wrapped in the night is a jest we embrace,
In the chaos of wonder, we find our place.

In Search of Hidden Truths

With magnifying glasses, we seek what we crave,
Hunting for answers, like treasure we brave.
Yet the truth wears a mask, it giggles and hides,
As we trip over riddles, and laughter collides.

We scribble down questions on napkins and maps,
Searching for wisdom in strange little gaps.
But the more that we dig, the more we're confused,
With every wild answer, we feel even more bruised.

In the maze of our minds, we stumble and fall,
Hatching ideas like birds in a hall.
Logic's a prankster, it dances away,
While we chase after knowledge, like cats at play.

So let's toast to confusion, and all its delight,
In the quest to unravel what's wrong and what's right.
For woven in chaos, with snippets of truth,
Is a funny old secret, just waiting for sleuths.

The Enigma of the Everyday

Oh, look at the splendor in a cereal bowl,
A morning routine with a twinkling soul.
How does toast land butter-side up every time?
Is breakfast a wizard or just quite sublime?

In the mundane dance of our daily grind,
We find strange oddities, feelings entwined.
The sock that goes missing, the keys on the roam,
In this circus of nonsense, we all find a home.

With tea leaves and fortune, we sip on our fate,
Wondering how our choices can be so ornate.
Each blink and each hiccup, a curious jest,
In the enigma of now, we're simply blessed.

So here's to the weird, the wacky, the fun,
As we navigate puzzles, of everyone.
May we laugh at the questions and embrace the absurd,
For every small mystery is a gift, that's confirmed.

Reflections of a Wandering Soul

In a mirror, I saw my face,
Wondering if I'd run the race.
Do I laugh, or do I cry?
The reflection winks, oh my!

With pockets full of silly dreams,
I chase after elusive beams.
A squirrel stole my sandwich treat,
Is this how I admit defeat?

I ponder life's great jesting ways,
Each twist and turn deserves a praise.
So I giggle at the absurd,
And let my thoughts become a word.

Through winding roads and sleepy towns,
I frolic free, defying frowns.
With every step, I trip and glide,
A comical, whimsical ride!

The Language of the Unsung

They say silence speaks the loudest tune,
Yet I prefer my kazoo in June.
With every honk, and every toot,
I summon joy, I wear a suit!

Whispers of thoughts hang in the air,
But I muster giggles without a care.
If laughter's a language, I'm fluent,
My heart, it dances, how resilient!

When I stumble over secret signs,
Belly laughs are my favorite pines.
Each signal leads to silly quests,
With rhymes that make me feel the best.

In forgotten corners, mischief strays,
Every chuckle captures sunny rays.
Unwritten words escape my tongue,
In the symphony of the unsung!

A Tapestry Unraveled

In threads of gold and deep maroon,
My story weaves a silly tune.
Each stitch a misadventure bold,
A tapestry that won't be sold.

I drop my yarn, it rolls away,
Chasing it, I trip and sway.
Each knot recalls a funky plight,
I laugh until I see the light.

Through mismatched patterns, I explore,
Life's fabric, full of folklore!
A patch of joy in every flaw,
Creating patterns, hold the awe!

So if you see my work unfold,
Join the dance, be wild, be bold.
We're all just threads in a grand design,
Let's stitch our laughs, they always shine!

The Fabric of Uncertainty

What's the blueprint for today?
A tangle of threads in disarray.
I wear mismatched socks with pride,
Who cares if they won't coincide?

Unruly seams create a laugh,
I can't predict my other half.
With every step, a new surprise,
I wink at fate, wear funny ties.

The fabric twists, it pulls, it strains,
Yet in the chaos, joy remains.
With every quirk, I dance and sway,
A patchwork pie of bright cliché.

In the loom of life, we all entwine,
Embrace the weird, let colors shine.
For in the cloth of what's unknown,
We find the fun, never alone!

Threads of the Unknown

In a world where socks just disappear,
We search for answers year by year.
The cat knows something, with a wink,
As we ponder over missing pink.

We chase our tails in circles tight,
While chasing dreams in the pale moonlight.
The toaster burns toast, an artful feat,
Yet not one peep from our breakfast treat.

Staring at clouds, we pose and muse,
What are they saying? We can't refuse.
The ice cream truck plays a catchy tune,
What if it's all just a cosmic cartoon?

In shadows where mysteries creep and crawl,
We laugh at the puzzles, come one, come all.
For in every riddle, a giggle we find,
Is perhaps the grand secret, of humankind.

The Riddle of Our Days

Morning coffee, a ritual we share,
With a side of the unknown—a puzzling affair.
What's that sound? Is it made by a ghost?
Or just my neighbor, loud and boast?

The weather's a joker, it laughs at our plans,
One minute it's sun, then rain with no bans.
Yet through all the chaos, we splatter and play,
Painting our worries a pastel bouquet.

Life's like a sitcom, vibrant and loud,
With laughter and tears, we're often enshrouded.
The punchline comes just when you least expect,
In the grand show of life, we're all the perfect wreck.

We juggle our fears, like clowns on a stage,
In the circus of each day, we laugh through the rage.
So let's toast to tomorrow with a wink and a grin,
For puzzling is best when shared with a twin.

Echoes of Forgotten Paths

Down dusty roads where shadows play,
We lose our keys, then laugh all day.
The squirrels know secrets tucked in their cheeks,
While we're scratching our heads, feeling like freaks.

We wander round corners, crumbling and old,
Searching for treasures, whispers of gold.
Yet all we find is a rusty old sign,
Pointing to places we can't quite define.

Tick-tock goes time, a mischievous mate,
Hiding our birthdays, just tempting our fate.
Did I just age? Or is it all a ruse?
A comedy script that we all must choose?

Yet still we dance through the mist of confusion,
Waving at echoes, crafting our illusion.
And in every giggle that bounces off walls,
We catch a glimpse of life's carnival balls.

The Unwritten Tapestry

In a loom of stories yet to be made,
We weave with laughter, bright threads displayed.
The patterns emerge as we stumble through,
Spinning our yarns with a wink or two.

What color is fortune? A question we ask,
While donning our quirks like a curious mask.
Life's not a thread but a snarl of fun,
Twisted and tangled but always on the run.

We stitch up our dreams on fabric of air,
And roll our eyes at fate's tricky lair.
Sewing up laughter, we hide all our fears,
In a blanket of joy, shared through the years.

So let's grab our needles, to poke and to prod,
At the humor that dances like a cheeky little god.
For in every strand, there's a giggle, a twist,
In the masterpiece of chaos, let's simply exist.

Tides of the Human Experience

We paddle in the ocean deep,
With rubber ducks and dreams to keep.
The waves of whimsy toss us about,
We giggle and laugh, never in doubt.

The shore is lined with sunscreen jars,
While we pretend to count the stars.
Crabs scuttle by with funky dance,
In this wild, wacky water-lovers' romance.

Each wave a riddle, tickles our toes,
Where wisdom's wave tops take off their clothes.
Fun awaits with every splash,
As we ride the surf of truth, in a dash.

So grab your floats and hold on tight,
Adventure awaits, both day and night.
In this sea of joy, one thing is clear,
We're simply here to have good cheer!

The Whirlwind of Existence

Around we twirl, in gusts we spin,
Life's like a dance, where we laugh and grin.
With wind in our hair, we're swept off our feet,
In a chaotic waltz, our hearts skip a beat.

We sip our drinks from cups that leak,
While juggling thoughts, we let out a squeak.
The world's a carnival, zany and bright,
We ride the Ferris wheel, soaring to heights.

As balloons float up, our worries collide,
In this crazy whirlwind, we're on a ride.
With cotton candy dreams swirling us 'round,
We find our joy where laughter is found.

So strap in tight, it's a rollercoaster twist,
In the name of fun, let's add to the list.
We're swirling, we're twirling, as friends do what's right,

Life's just a party, in day and night!

Portraits of an Unfolding Mystery

Canvas of curiosity, brushes dance bright,
Each stroke a giggle, a chuckle in sight.
Paint splats ask why the sky's not green,
And who made the chocolate-flavored protein.

We sketch our days with crayons and chalk,
Where doodles of cats in pajamas can talk.
The shapes are quirky, the colors ask more,
As we paint our stories from ceiling to floor.

In jigsaw puzzles, the pieces don't fit,
Yet in this chaos, we find a sweet wit.
With raised eyebrows, we drink from cups,
Filled with questions that bubble and sup.

So strike a pose, let mystery unfold,
In this gallery of glee, be brave, be bold.
With laughter in frames and joy in the air,
We embrace the strange, with a colorful flair!

The Secret Garden of Thoughts

In a garden where giggles blossom and grow,
We plant little seeds of wisdom, a row.
Worms tell jokes in the soil so deep,
While fairies play hide-and-seek but never creep.

The sunbeams tickle the flowers awake,
While butterflies giggle and tease the snake.
With petals of laughter, we water with cheer,
Growing ideas that bring us near.

Beehives hum with stories untold,
As we wander this path, both timid and bold.
We dance with the daisies, we twirl with the breeze,
In this whimsical place, we're wholly at ease.

So gather your thoughts, let your worries depart,
In this secret garden, we'll share from the heart.
With joy like wildflowers bursting in bloom,
We'll laugh in this realm, dispelling all gloom!

The Secret Handshake of the Universe

With cosmic winks and nods we play,
The stars giggle in their cheeky way.
Galaxies swirl, a dance so grand,
But what's the password? No one understands.

Comets dash, like kids at play,
In this riddle game, they lead astray.
Black holes yawn, their secrets keep,
While meteors giggle as they leap.

We twist our mustaches, adjust our hats,
In this wacky wonder, we're clumsy cats.
The universe chuckles, a celestial joke,
As we scratch our heads, and hope for a poke.

But in this chaos, there's fun to find,
Laughter echoes, and binds our kind.
So let's raise a toast, with a wink and a glance,
To the universe's secret, a whimsical dance!

Companions on an Infinite Quest

We wander far, with socks that don't match,
With snacks in our pockets, a sandwich to catch.
Through space's vastness, we roam hand in hand,
Discovering wonders, unplanned and unscanned.

The moon gives a chuckle, the sun throws a grin,
As we trip over stardust, and slip in a spin.
Our quest is peculiar, a riddle in flight,
As we chase after meaning, like it's a kite.

Planets roll by, like balls in a game,
They tease us with riddles, but nothing's the same.
We make a pact, to never grow old,
And laugh at the stories that space has told.

As fellow explorers, we'll share in the fun,
With giggles and grins, until day is done.
So here's to the journey, with all its mischief,
Companions forever, in cosmic relief!

Unfolding the Scroll of Existence

With scrolls so ancient, we twist and we turn,
Hunting for secrets, for wisdom we yearn.
We laugh at the scribbles, the ink's gone astray,
As time plays tricks, in a silly ballet.

Each fold is a puzzle, a wink from the past,
With jokes hidden slyly, so bright and so vast.
We untangle threads, with giggles and flair,
As the map to the mysteries leads us somewhere.

The scroll rolls away, like a dance too wild,
And we chase after meanings, like a curious child.
With laughter our compass, we sail through the scroll,
Finding treasures of wisdom that tickle the soul.

So here we stand, with our laughter and cheer,
Unfolding the mysteries, year after year.
The scroll may be long, with riddles galore,
But with friends by our side, we'll always explore!

Resonance of the Unknown

In echoes of silence, we hear a faint laugh,
The unknown tickles, as we sketch a new path.
We dance with the shadows, in a curious way,
With giggles and antics, we brighten the day.

Waves of confusion, they wobble and sway,
Like jelly on plates, they lead us astray.
But we take it in stride, with humor and glee,
The unknown's a trickster, oh, don't you agree?

With each little riddle, we circle around,
Finding joy in the chaos, in laughter we're bound.
The universe chuckles, like a playful friend,
In the resonance of gaffes that never do end.

So here's to the laughter within the unknown,
To the quirks of the cosmos that we've brightly shone.
In a world full of puzzles, let's sing and we'll shout,
For the joy of this mystery, that's what it's about!

The Language of the Unfathomable

In riddles we speak, like cats in hats,
Chasing tales, like acrobatic rats.
Knots in our brains, oh what a mess,
Try to untangle, I must confess.

With winks and smirks, the puzzles bloom,
Like socks in a dryer, they dance and zoom.
We laugh at the chaos, what a delight,
Playing charades in the dark of night.

A whisper of wisdom lies in the jest,
Unraveling truths that we try to nest.
Like toddlers in mud, we squirm and play,
Beneath the surface, odd games we sway.

In giggles we find the profound and the strange,
Each question a jest, each thought a range.
So pour a drink, let's toast absurdity,
For in our confusion lies true maturity.

Portrait of an Elusive Dream

In colors that swirl, our dreams take flight,
Dressed up like clowns in the pale moonlight.
They hide in the corners, giggling with glee,
Whispering secrets only they can see.

Like chasing rainbows or catching a breeze,
We stumble through moments like wobbly knees.
With every good laugh comes a new silly quest,
For trophies of nonsense, we give it our best.

Our hopes are like jelly, wobbly and bright,
Take a spoonful—oh, what a sight!
Craving clarity birthed from the haze,
Yet every attempt turns out to be a maze.

With jest and laughter, we paint with our fears,
Tickling our worries until they disappear.
The portrait may shift, but the laughter remains,
As we wander through dreams playing delightful games.

The Cloak of Illusion

Draped in a cloak of shimmering quirks,
We strut through the world with comical smirks.
Behind the fabric, what secrets reside?
We laugh when the truth chooses to hide.

An onion of layers, we peel it with care,
Finding funny faces beneath the glare.
Each wrinkle tells tales we just can't ignore,
As we fumble through stories that always implore.

In marbles and puzzles, the answers dissolve,
Playful and tricky, no problems to solve.
So throw off that garment, let laughter reveal,
The joy in the chaos, the ridiculous deal.

The fabric of wisdom is silly, it seems,
Stitched with the threads of our oddest dreams.
With giggles as currency, we barter away,
For questions that tickle, we're happy to play.

Beyond the Horizon of Certainty

In the land of what-ifs, we frolic and run,
Building our castles, oh isn't it fun?
With maps made of jelly and guides gone astray,
We dance on the edges of humor's ballet.

A compass of giggles, it spins in delight,
Leading us onward, from morning to night.
Each step taken lightly, with caution in jest,
The horizon ahead, a puzzling quest.

We're sailors of nonsense, we hoist up the sail,
Navigating through jokes on a whimsical trail.
With horizons uncharted, we find bittersweet,
In laughter and questions, we're blissfully fleet.

So here's to the journey, however it twists,
Each moment a riddle, each laugh on our lists.
The shore may be blurry, but let's take a chance,
For the joy in the mystery is life's lovely dance.

www.ingramcontent.com/pod-product-compliance
Lightning Source LLC
Chambersburg PA
CBHW051637160426
43209CB00004B/689